The Waker's Corridor

| POEMS |

THE WAKER'S CORRIDOR

JONATHAN THIRKIELD

Louisiana State University Press
Baton Rouge

Published by Louisiana State University Press
Copyright © 2009 by Jonathan Thirkield
All rights reserved
Manufactured in the United States of America

An LSU Press Paperback Original
FIRST PRINTING

Designer: Michelle A. Neustrom
Typeface: Bank Gothic, Chaparral Pro
Printer and binder: Thomson-Shore, Inc.

LIBRARY OF CONGRESS CATALOGING-IN-PUBLICATION DATA

Thirkield, Jonathan, 1973–
    The waker's corridor : poems / Jonathan Thirkield.
        p. cm.
    ISBN 978-0-8071-3441-2 (pbk. : alk. paper)
    I. Title.
    PS3620.H57W35 2009
    811'.6—dc22
                                    2008042024

The author thanks the editors of those publications in which the following poems appeared:
American Letters & Commentary: "Mystery Plays I–V"; *Barrow Street:* "Your Journey (4:111)";
The Canary: "Auf Naxos," "Commedia dell'arte (14:114)"; *Colorado Review:* "Abend (10:101)";
jubilat: "The Tragedians (29:51)"; *New American Writing:* "Design for a Silver Box in the Shape
of a Melon, 1918"; *New Orleans Review:* "New York New York"; *1913: A Journal of Forms:* "White
Coves," "Mystery Plays X, XII"; *Verse:* "The Mourners (44:44)"; *Volt:* "Upstate (7:127)"; *Web
Conjunctions:* "Elegy," "Fatherland."

The author also wishes to thank everyone at the University of Iowa and the Academy of
American Poets for their support. My thanks to Linda Bierds and Mark Levine. Thanks to
LSU Press. Thanks to the sodal. And a very special thank you to Chris Chen.

The paper in this book meets the guidelines for permanence and durability of the Committee
on Production Guidelines for Book Longevity of the Council on Library Resources. ∞

For Ema

CONTENTS

I

WAKING IN THREE LANDS

Fatherland

An Elegy

I. Streamside

A perfect scene: a voice unwarrantedly
sweet exiting the shade: a man's red mouth
rough cheeks white skin: in wood—a gondolier
plays the scattered pieces of his fiddle-form
in broken light and audience estranged
from living sound: but sweetly arcs his song:
with the innocent abandon of a child
sleepwalking in his father's nightshirt
he calls us into him: the sky a crowd
of filaments: the waving anthers itch
the tree: silver moths: a white fabric cast
over the wall above his chest: a still
life of pears grapes lilacs other flora:
Robert is my father he sings opera

II. Children with Flashlights

So the torches fly to him
so we run the lights' small
radii around our feet: roots
catching the arcs: breaking the
the rings and rings around us:
cloths against the phosphorus
organs: walling the surround:
woods up bear up the liquid in the
top sky glass: soil in it turns
the upside world to shadow shows:
blue-gray lawn: damp dawn for
head lamps: and flying as with
wine into the dark glass of him

III. Under the Proscenium

Play: play speechless on the springs wild and
watered woods red hares play out in gray gags
under the mark and mask: palsy a plum in a basket
with his strung speech shuddering: how easy it is
to stray in the parts of an actor's life:
move the angel over the child's head like this
and in his likeness though wooden it works
wonders without words: all is here for hiding:
he never was himself: we crowd in him:
icebulbs gathering on bluebells: woods
falling in a cicatrix of water: sugar to cake
this petal: this April snow: this winter
reclaims his sweetened life: the buds
recoiling in the shock of its art
show us that pain is candy on the harp

IV. What Children Learn

Now sing in place: but low as to a sleeping
child or love or: sing in place of me
but with your mouth against a wall into
the floor or into water as the moon
does: frozen over frozen youth with blue
tide curving over those young eyes: it's painless
a dream of fatherland: two of us running
down the head: stream after stream recycling all
until it all seems suddenly so still:
an endless afternoon descends on you:
so you look up to see the trees' bare fruit:
you are still growing on the hill:
you'll sleep better knowing how it tastes:
there is a bitterness being awake

V. The Insect King

A clicking stone: it rests on eyes a touch
too wet but drying: opening a blink
then shutting: sticking each time to itself:
a beetle eating grapes:
he's under the piano with a green
one buried down there: will you come and play?
everything begs for an accompaniment:
the bench is dusted but the phantom-limbed
musician won't arrive or if he does
what strength is left for fingering the keys?
Try my clumsy music on the insect:
one low note and he pauses with a click:
lost: relishing in the echo: he grows
peaceful: and then resumes as he's supposed

VI. Winter Carries over Summer

No melting in July now: no mourning songs
one tracing water dries: one wilting writes:
O singular jongleur sing: from noise crowded
on small yellow leaves fall elegies:
turn a season's woods to still columns:
learn a myth perching the nightingales:
rehearse your madness so when it comes I
can still love. Is that possible?
Either madness or a heart stopped ends
love: words fill darkly with a world and songs
empty themselves into this type: this real
strain of sickness: more characters to line
the minds of children following their parents
to a still place where love is just resistance.

VII. Song

There was a myth of innocence:
a boy and carpenter would dance
together on an almond stage
constructed for the marriage
of the boy's mother and a god
(or possibly an invalid
who promised money in return)
she let her modest orchard burn
to clear the hillside for a ring
surrounded by fresh garlanding
prosceniums to stand above
a painted sea and orchestra
but her betrothed disappeared
left son and wood and carpenter

VIII. Son

"What change is in your pockets?" I, the grave-
robber asked. I set a peach on the landing.
It withered with the rest. Pillows paved
the yard. Light, as feathers, fell, lightly candling
us at the feet of stars. The unearthed earth
cooled up on me, and while I was unsleeving
your jacket to give it some of my warmth,
I said, "Exactly eighteen years of grieving
must mean something." I double-checked my watch.
No one was here. The sleeves with flesh pink lining
fell damp and cold. I went to fetch the peach
I'd left when I was twelve years old. "Remind me,
what does anything mean?" sang old Robert
the dysphoric beneath the willow tree.

IX. Memory

Quiet me: show me a landing in the woods
where he is painting: a tree arched above
as if it holds him up with strings:
he makes the stairs from stumps climbing the gray
brush tinting the low hill and plasters ice
on the slats and roof: over the windows
he draws a blank and bottomless horizon:
we become him in July: we cover the inside
with sheets: run on the porch as if on stage
and speak only to the tree: when ice
separates from its leaves: with pinhole pipes
forming as the water drains: it sings wind
through every narrow corridor of breath in
you: life a shiver: a brush clinks in the tin

X. Ice Sheet

Push on the frozen thing: and you *will* change.
Fingers warm: empty their warmth on slight dents:
wet finger-rests for notes on a recorder.
Press longer and clear sockets open outward:
they taper at the edges: barely gaining depth:
I look for eyes in a hollow: I look for music
on the window: tears under the rug
and a stream nowhere: soon enough I'll drain
this hand completely: I'll be numb: it's useless:

How can you make the dead cry.
I'm breaking my room. The cement dried
recording the hand of an absentminded child
or parts of the face of an older man's head.

XI. Father's Song

I had a clock it woke all day
in hiccuped white embattled cries
I broke my glasses on the street
to blind my sense of dignity
and wrapped the sheets as knocking on
a filmy door as knocking on
a rough body of water
a dust sheet pinned over
a soft pedal organ I once
moaned long over life
and my palm fitted most
of my son it was as if
some discord kept my feet airborne
and my head planted down in quartz

Abendland

trans. The Occident, the West
lit. Land of Evening

In Köln, each triangle picks at the dome; spines work their way, out of the scaffolds and stainless girders, into spires.

A brown even sky with light fixtures in the dents; her mouth overlaid by a few beads of frost on the train window in transit.

The station's metal wrists. Traced white with snow. A ministry of interstice. Of atoms tensed inside a crystal lattice.

The fiberglass shudders. She holds down his knee to steady them. Pins the other against the side rail. You were sleeping.

Are we there?

We pass as two shapes may assume a form of love. If just in passing. In the seats across a slender man bends over a book placed

At his knees. His daughter rests a flashlight on his shoulder, her ear pressed firmly to his jaw. Should he be whispering?

A tree. Lit momentarily in the passing. Train lights. Quickly it grows. Ductile. And cannot hold to its shape. What sound

Now grows with you? I am not standing. In a steel extension of when snow. Was not heavy before metal. But light on one spoon.

The overlook passes. The cathedral arrows. From the small lungs inside her. A coughing; it crowns. To the rounded south.

THE WAKER'S CORRIDOR

Night radiates in spills of survival whose breath
is a room, on the mantle a mirror,
the same child each time—
Rhine passages on his sleeve, the eye
of a bird always behind him.
Steady, even

Hear the trembling hold a singed note. I told my mouth,
Close.
A child can imagine anything
when he doesn't know: paper globe,
a tapered star, a storm
upends the curtains, life lights in
across the low apartments facing
breadthways: the street, the stream, the sea, the sound
all cut too broad to designate
a seam, where bare
trees mediate
the crossing images.

Branches weave over a woman, distributing
her
in parts:
a marble counter; hand and forearm stir;
dark parted hair on her forehead;
a bare foot taps the tiles to music
unheard from where you stand;
in her left hand, there is an egg:
it moves under
the veil of trees to an aperture,
a simple white bowl of German design.
She knocks the shell
against the bowl's sharp, turned-in cusp
(one hand still stirs)
a crescent crack smiles out
with yolk and silk
to mix among the whisk's
thickening foam.

Her home is low and close to us, so close the eyes
can't
help but
break the view:
tall windows, trees, and the woman across
the way making breakfast for us
at night when something loud woke the youngest,
something far outside, far above
that thundered in the way
machines do, without a building,
rising rumble,
but in an immediate crash beginning all
the lesser sounds, small cymbals clashing
under a higher cloud, and then the storm
as if beckoned
by the first note plays its patters on the sills
becalming the uncertainty:
it was thunder.
That's what it seems she says
to reassure the child or herself:
"It was thunder.
Don't worry, the rain proves
it was thunder."
She starts up in a rush to get the windows closed.

☙

One latch and a fever brought crossing waves, iron,
gales, waterways,
occidental music
in the lion's
hair strings, tin mouths rattling over silver
cups. Push—and the bellows
accordion
out, riding, gap-mouthed, the mountain
crests, the Oxus through the Wakhan Corridor,
west a gravel-
black woods, a cracked hearth's lintel syruped in

fat, a narrow strip where Poles commute
to the Baltic cleared out in a breath of pure sym-
metry—white, toothed
love. At home the blood knows nothing
more than the rise and fall
of its sugar, and far echo
the drains of an alpine source pouring routes
when Persia drew the mind's limits,
and rivers turned to borders when we sang,
image to
image-
hinge,
until all thought a human form bathed within them.

On the inhale,
on the first inhale of
an instrument,
a deserted street lined
parallel with
the Hudson fills with sand. A beach
day, a beach day!
School is canceled. The children play till dusk
under the loving watch of seagulls.
A sound of waves,
a shuttered distance from the sea,
travels through the tall glass
universe of things, a harbor, a screen,
and lands for less than a moment
inside a lighted shell. Hear it asking,
What is
yours?
And listen, the person next to you is coughing.

In the evening, she wakes
right beside me,
not knowing if
to talk. Gardens below, still lit
by a few windows, cast a polished stalk

or two across the outgrowths of light.
What sacrifice or innocence
can you produce within
your weld-white substance? She who sleeps
faithfully beside me /like a marble
egg/
fallen to a mountain hill /from a chestnut tree.

One spilling light
to hold us in a child's spell—
He is won with a world of despair,
And is lost with a toy—
In the form of a boy, anonymous
as a yellowing room, a spoon holding an egg.

DESIGN FOR A SILVER BOX IN THE SHAPE OF A MELON, 1918

after Peche

In sheet metal or silver shallows
filled with these:
hollow, floating
where some assumed votives
would be lit. Or
lanterns.

Do you see the time of day? With still
some red to
flush the waders,
scatter against a few
boats, and fire
cannons

Distantly, first. When we see the flare,
we listen.
Sand buries at
our ankles. They appear,
the apples or
melons

Printed along the wallpaper, half
submerged in
their setting, brushed
dark with stems, the silver
flats folded in
fans. Too

Many of the waders grasp the stem
and pull off
the top of an
apple or melon, so
the base fills with
water

And sinks. Silver leaves from the stem. One
small woman's
pearl earring drops
like so many others
in the shallows.
Eardrops.

I met a woman in Viennese
glass. What was
in her jewel case?
A shade that turns over
a blue trellis.
Flower

Theater (or garden) on the flattened
silver wall,
a gray screen where
boats fire, the blush falls
and dyes a cherry
chime.

White Coves

NEW YORK NEW YORK

A runnel forks at a patch of wild lilies.
As day drains the monochrome.
Shade from the mountains.
It is just me.
And him for the day.
A creek below that we can only hear.
A film goes up against the sky.
My son climbs on the roof.
Why all the dust, son?
So I can be your eyes.
So green even in the fall, everything abend.
What can you see up there?
I see you in the moss.
I see a bobtail rushing uphill.
And the stone?
No stone from here.
The leaves block it.
Come down now, you might slip.
I will never slip.
I will never slip.
I think he is dancing to it.
I am not worried.
The runnel forks at a patch of wild lilies.
The distance is a dance.
Soon the brown leaves will hold their edges in its water.
Soon we will all move.
Downhill, downstate, together.
One girl carries a housecat in her basket.
One keeps stopping to tie your shoes.
One keeps her skirt from dragging the earth along with her.
Come down.
I'm not going anywhere.

Still embrace your beautiful land, and still of your daughters, O Father,
Of your islands, the flowering, not one has been taken.

I.

There is, beneath, a promise of renewal.
The workers' pavement poured on outgrowths: squares,
Once raised or pushed askew by roots and cracked
By constant pressure, restlessness, by night

Were harmonized. First, Twelfth was closed. They cast
The worklights high above the Tudor houses.
The mixers cycled in their noise through
The quiet hours, while residents would sleep

With their ears covered. First, a rising smoke,
Pale white, passed by the windows. Cutting through
The old cement took time. But quickly they
Discarded every vestige, shard by shard:

The blots of cast off chewing gum that stuck
And turned to tar. The unintentional
Designs embedded in the tin and glass
(One piece beneath a corbeil might have been

The flat, diluted outline of a bowl
With arching flowers). The initials drawn
With sticks by two young sisters when
The old cement took forever to dry.

All these were hauled off to the harbor dump.
And in their place a scent of chloride washed
The air. The spreader boxes kept each square
Minutely even, white, in perfect mean.

For many nights the lights would move from street
To street. And morning, in its uniform
Brightness, unveiled the clean geometry.
And as this order crept along the ground

Restlessly, we waited far away.

II.

It is a slow spring. The sashes open.
He ties them down with linen, then takes
a few moments to engage his mistress.

Should she be drinking from a pickle jar?
Or piercing olives with his daughters' earrings?
No matter. It's Sunday. The martinis are dry.

Finally quiet, except the gifted child
at the house next door, playing a sonata.
"What will you give me now?" He watches

Her fingers mimic the notes on one of the girls'
bedposts. Her face is lightly powdered. Her robe
is opened down the middle. "You are a bore."

Out in the country, the girls are a sum
of miles, decorative rows of windmills. Dormant.
They ossify in his mind. Which is which?

Today, the woman here, her flesh never stops
feeling unfamiliar. "What are their names,
again?" Sometimes it's as if they've grown

invisible. As if, like clouds, the day
passes through their willow skin. No matter.
He pictures them in white blouses, boarding

the ferry, dockworkers making overtures,
so many things that can happen outside
this house, this street, this block, this separation

of the rocks and sea growing like a wave
farewell. Somewhere will take them. No matter.
He is a bore. A flood. The barrel of a gun

points somewhere off the coast, waiting
to fire in celebration. A thousand times
the embers we turn over to the sea.

III. Lydia

The only one taken.
Atlantic or straits. Tantalum mines.

Her sleeve
dipped from mud to rock.

She swept leftovers
off a bone bridge:

salt cod, flour, paper sown
over the brined.

Bluefish scattered
over bitumen.

His ivory shoulder. Obstructed waves
lapped on clay

(or does a child in one's lap).
Blue sown keel.

Low arch lowered sail,
high sleeves.

A sailcloth wrapped.
The fishnets

hammock a litter.
Hold the stretched skin.

The moorings rubbed
dove gray.

At the waist, coves.

Cliffs edge
near tropopause

to flood blue
then flood white,
or green earth.

Lift or peel cloths
from wine, feathers

discarded by a chopping block.
Kidney pond,

steel cut.
The hymnal from square

brushed by the salt wall.
The hulls, lung filled.

Hall cloth. White worn
off the shoulder.

Ivory shoals.
Letted.

A cutlass handle mounted
upon bier and bark. As air beats

with sulfur
a boy

drinks himself white. A lifted shift
lights her knees.

Moon pulls on water,
on ankles.

One creel toppled.
One carved mouth from soapstone.

Indenture. No long option of solvents.
Girl weighted in glasswork.

Roseate. Hail pattern. Coast.

Amidst smoke and castanets,
claps on cattle skin

is fog, mine steam.
No stone squares here, but
a fluted circus.

Concentric,
echo to peal.

IV. Lilac (9:111)

Around me. They cannot be signaling from a window. Except the bowing voices. Which may be men. Have they been spreading potash again?

It sweetens the ground. Outside. Among the low attendance of cars. When at dusk insects break from their tight wrappings. It trills.

It rings. I ward the windpipes into populations strolling with the cicadas. Would I if I planted the window beneath me. Begin to molt?

The tiles are cold. It is at the wall. An arm's reach from the window. Where squares start bending toward. Safety is the promise of all.

Come out you. Listen. I circled my thoughts in onion skin with high colors. Blue. Maybe a withered blue. But so much of it seeps through

The skin. I pinned it to wall. You read. I am, for you in ink, the voice undressed. Tear this sheet from this whitewashed stone. Wear it!

The wall produces some dandelions in response. Call them sunflowers. Call the mothers. Who come in white covers to undress the wall.

Do they carry loaves under their arms? No. Do they make each floor a widow's walk? Maybe they are still cleaners reeling the pulley and

Lowering themselves slowly. As water drips from the scaffold. To my sill. Outside. A small breeze works hard to unfold. My white gown

Boat toy boat law boat low in Melodie's arms. She blows green water
ripples, she squeezes humming blots from bows, her lungs. She goes

No. No honey. She bolts high birds filled with fancy over her pale
Melodie. Now darling leave, let it set. Let it boat now. Mother links

Me, Melodie lapsed on a string. The watches are stirring with scissors.
Low boats in the sing. She bleats and she pushes the paper pink

Boat, sail first, into green. It swallows her fists. The water is thick. With
boats seasick with boats. Where lime dyes eddy she rows.

II

UNDER THE PROSCENIUM

AUGUST'S VOICE: *They won't hurt you. You were dreaming.*
KIRSTEN'S VOICE: *They were talking.*
AUGUST'S VOICE: *They're only shadows.*
KIRSTEN'S VOICE: *They were talking.*
AUGUST'S VOICE: *Shhhh.*
KIRSTEN'S VOICE: *They were talking.*

—LANFORD WILSON, *The Mound Builders*

We the Dark Characters

The mental institution was funny. The way the mad are funny. From the cement recreation area. She could not see beyond the figures. Left by felled trees.

Now the far trees reminded a patient of Tangiers. While on walks. She formed a basket from her shirt. Held the end away from her belly. Placed pinecones in

The light. Cotton hammock. The orderly disposed of her shells when they started. To spill out from under her bed. The hallways were colored an off-white

That lacked a tan or gray tinge. One patient couldn't stand. The sight of yellow. His mother painted his child that color. When he was stationed in Korea.

When there was laughter. It was a funny laughter. As if it begged to hear a joke. (Knock knock.) When a visitor meets his father in a beige room he should not

Recognize. Him this thin and sleepless.
                                        Children are funny. One
parent removes (himself). And a boy forgets his voice. And pictures
only a tin Napoleon

Statue. A photograph of a striped and collared shirt. Eyes whose green has worn dim. Are set deeply. Can always grow more tired. I say the building sinks.

April (Sorrow) holds above her head
a tipped amphora, draining water first
against her ash-blonde hair, and then
into a basin made of the same stone as she.
When April calls the statue "April," Ling,
administering a Flower-Acid Peel,
says, "Shut," and softly pins her client's lips
together, "Tight." The peel, extracted from
Hibiscus flowers, works into the skin.
To lighten hyperpigmentation, Ling
applies a second film to April's shroud,
and turns the background music slightly loud:
The Velvet Underground's "Stephanie Says"
in candy coated static. A Japanese
chanteuse unfolds the tune in a high pitch.
She has to go.

      A child too off-white
to lie beneath the sun in Belarus
plays Tetris by a row of green umbrellas.
His father thumbs *Ecrits* by Jacques Lacan,
and tunes the radio to Chaka Khan.
I feel for you.

      Sweet lord, you play me false.
The showers work like strings leading my limbs
into the ocean. Only once, when you
had me undo my bonnet, then my blouse,
and called me Miranda, I wet myself.
You said you were a swan.

COMMEDIA DELL'ARTE (15:52)

In fractions I, blessed
and left of the stairwell,
am forging.
>   Tim regained his sight
>   only partially . . . the longer
>   part hid.
One back, I leapt
into the channel, where now
he was measured in
>   His speech. What passed
>   for life? A clown
>   noised in his palace.
Friend, you have the wrong
tie. Off the steps
to the Romanesque
>   Chancery, I handed
>   weather sticks—
>   to the thinnest boarders.
Place a lid upon the light.
A dime shaken
off my eyes. A counter-
>   Pane of running
>   figures spread over Jane .
>   and me. While we slept
Time moved
my abbess to tears . . . that I left
is what I don't see.
>   What he might divine—reaching
>   with a stick
>   for daybreak—dogs
Lost on the end of Bride.
Their only duration,
when long alarms
>   Crowd over their plots.
>   You've something sweet
>   on your mouth.

God what is yours:
the train gathering
on the isle. Wide ushers
      Convening, guarded
      about the bindings,
      the silent carnifex.
The blue forgets me.
Mary, your prophesy—
is rhymed . . . Edgar?

A tiger tears at a machine. A small train engine. Which I left on stage.
After cleansing her cage. We don't live here, Governor. So fine me.

My transparent house, a willow tree. Filled with oil from Hades. Friends.
In your paltry pots. Do you have enough? To still be my friends?

Under the tarpaulin. Under the dolphin sign. Gather round me.
Forgiving Columbine. Brief beings in a caravan. Sown to the white
ground.

Listen to her. She with the letter opener at her throat. "First there was
the Fainter (the Artist) the cosmetically ruled and slim female

"Celebrity." She beckons the men. Shaking her beads. "She makes a
happy jingle off her dress. She's the beauty we'll be catching when she

"Falls dramatically. Five years of attentive guests. Slept at the doors of
her dressing room, wishing, with jewels, to be her dressers—

"In her drawers. Next was the Faster. Bloated, despite herself." My stalk
of Columbine sucks her rouged cheeks in. Then puffs them wide.

"With child. The father and a panther sleep by bars—just too closely
spaced for her to pass." Listen underneath her chest. It's all real.

"By days in the weaving room, admiring the clear hairs surrounding her
navel and the clear hairs darkening on her child's head, she filed

"The abrasions on her cuticles with straw torn from a basket, and salved
them with concubine oil. This was the Crier." Oh poor Columbine!

Your words are numbering. As bells that cricket out the worst news. Now
turn our thoughts to bangers and to mash. Does the Lover come next?

"Only the lover who comes in a card. I can count the characters on my
fingers. The final one, Patience in a hospital bed, views widows haply

"Exiting the home," (There'll be a collection at the end.) "till she disappears from herself, as a blue bottle from the self. And I become

"Half who she is and all who she was." What's then the partition 'tween you and you and she? What will you pay? My characters play the bones.

A bout of grief whirrs the priest i'the rib cage. A numb lark on

A copper bough warms, with currents, his feet. Now he can feel

A single singing thing scratched and scratched in digits far

From boyhood through a wrongheaded grave. The way the search

Party went out, it's too far to retrace your entrance, mouths

The lark. A trail of ruddy wine on his cheeks stales. Swiftly,

He grasps the roots, and unearths a cinema among the spinets:

Spirits cast pure images. Ice spins in from the lake's edges.

Of dead forms Father is the stillest. No passages crossing by

Light or a struck wire. He is so surprised to feel anything now

That he has triggered a trap with his figures. His hand asleep

On the plectrum, the players hold every life in a single minor

Key. Simple choice fills the forests with noise. I am certain

We're lost from looking at the frost on every fallen curtain.

I saw much happier parties traveling across the same current

As the lark. They feed a wounded deer and loose their children

Into a catalogue of trees. So sure they will return. These are

Dressed as well as you and I. They suffer the same, brief bouts

Of sickness. But they feel more deeply. They see more clearly

The images before them as pieces of their hearts plucked by an

Innocent. Frail hand. A voice parched. A parent stammering,

Passing through the hard ground. Moving into a peaceful age.

Spring. The lakes fill up with families. All know each other.

The children swim and learn the names of birch, knotted pine.

Every new town overlooking the woods is building us a church.

If we could see steeples through trees. Instead of following

The lark's nourishing maze of ruined wires. We'd find our way

Leaving our ancestors as characters in luminous jars buried

Under the thorn thickets. To finish our days with the living.

They are music done. Bodies of shale. Heads of eaves.

A husband's rendering in stone. He slept in thieves'

Garments in a visitors house in town burnt by the time

Of day when the west room's window irons striped him.

Three psalter flower tops had broken from the garden

Like children. "You weed like an hysterical woman,"

They said. The ruddy, horizon-filtered sun blotted

The town square as if it were a prone colossus sotted,

Face down and drenched with wine. His elbows sagged,

The steeples cast gray teeth that softened the edges

Between beginnings of brush, a stoppage of commerce

At seven and, crossing the two, the unsteady hearse—

A bridge's unfinished ridges shivering its wheels—

Baring an imperfect death to an unremarkable field.

There weren't enough criers at the time. So some fled

At any unexpected sound. Much of the train dwindled.

A modest flood uphill. When they reached the gallows

Hooded widows wooded the meadow with their shadows,

A statue of an angel strangely strangled angled over

The crossbeam seemed strung up by ivy—acting a lover

Climbing from his bed to twist his arm around the neck

And shoulders of his wife sitting up still and awake:

"The magpie in a Bruegel painting stands there where

A rope should be. Highest living thing not in the air.

Much lower, the peasants in a rondo dance. They dance

In threes, and couples gaze at knotted trees, a trace

Of excrement enlivening their noses. The gossiping

Gardens, sleeves wet from the beer tables, slipping

To my knees. It's a joke, dying. See the children leer

Under wash lines, one thieving an orange, a muscular

Orange, and hiding it down his pants to play a naughty

Resurrection game. Little pairs of girls in Germany

Throw dolls into a mid-Lent stream. Yes, they are all

Returning. All of them, lips wetted and sculptural,

Mouthing an enchanted syntax scripted in Romances.

The corpse minus a head, wasn't who we thought it was.

The wife gone twenty years, only hiding out of spite.

And Ariel, your shipwreck trick, with sweet sprites

Singing, fooled Ferdinand fully. Can you hear them?

The neighbors in a thin packet of light trying themes

On each other. One is your father. Are you listening?

'Pour me' 'What?' 'Some more—my heart is thinning.'

'First Roll. Hah! Hard eights!' 'Did you see a king go

By here?' 'Aches?' 'No, sorry.' 'Didn't think so.'"

The Landing

The Landing: An Island (45:33)

A swift rising in the air: poor, filmy on
the statue's sword or torch: red flower
in a hand downstream from where the neon

red umbrella wires the insurance tower
with an illusion: the building watches
over us: electric head turned downward

high over the landing planes the cracks
in sound falling in transparent stairs
all the way to the bottom of the air: wake

of quicklime ground glass schist glare
of a receding sun seen through a century
of elements torched, kiln-crazed: a tear

in a distant scaffold covering beneath
which a man slowly peels away at the fast
accretion of the past. A father dreams.

Or simply cleans the old wall so the rest
of us can pass below just a while longer,
without things falling unexpectedly.

And in the rooms we rise again for water,
or to get the ringing phones, or to check
on a child resting by a dormant radiator

in a narrow bed. You can see a figure walk
from time to time, today or twenty years
ago, as he brings down the covers tucked

around his child, as he touches his ears
red and damp from sleep, pose unaltered
as a school day goes by, lying as on a bier

unconvincingly. A palm waves, tilted,
throwing shadows on his lightly sanded
eyelids. He knows the game: who filters

Out life the longest wins.
                              Father lands
in the snow-colored carnival. One thin
chance of a world crosses the Atlantic.

Verrazzano rode the brilliant cut skin
of the bay, studying facet after facet.
The sun-built sparks jeweled his mind:

white cities, harbor-perched lancets
to cast a mirror image of the Florentine
villas that line the Arno. Down Spanish

coasts, on Madeiran rock, the Dauphine
launched. Is there speech or a language
where their voice is not heard? The line

that goes out through the earth to gauge
the distance from our homes never lands
on a fine point, but circuits to the end.

First Floor (3:185)

Safe winter sill. Blessed cockle shell. Carnations.
Blown frost weaves a glass vase. Silhouette
vellum flower stacks. Jet murex. Shower
salt, seaweed, ivory, coral off the legs
to the feet, unswept roots and rice seeds.

Muse in the webbed eyes for home. Fly indoors.
In nearest distance is a worn, preserved
sound of a horn attenuated through
thick, thick walls, crust. Sheets billow from the wheels'
patient crawl down dove sleeted streets.

From birth, this is how you see a city,
in the narrow time we were all awake,
from below, nested in a costrel neck
painted with birds, pedestrians, a tree
trunk steadied in thin iron, always
aware of the two rivers framing you.

Second Floor (3:185)

Ema's pouring water in the morning pitcher,
dressed in old shorts and a t-shirt too big for her,
waiting for the faucet to run cold enough,
nothing is heavy on her mind, the hair
she washed last night is still behaving enough.

Somehow, you're in a house that we forgot about,
a rock moated by a stream barely crawling
over the leaves. Is it a child then? Or is it
just the moss sticking to us? When is a mind
perfectly clear? Do your hands do all the feeling

for you? The temperature changes so slowly
that it feels the same. Each day feels the same
motion pouring over its skin. It's hard to tell
what she would say. A living one awaking.
In sitting light. A dust broom on a blue shelf.

Fourteenth Floor

101 Central Park West, 14F.
The children sleep in a wing to the left.
Tell us, when does the performance end?
Way past your bedtime, the fifth act goes till twelve.
Your doctor's bag? Your cigarette? It was
half hanging off the chest beside your cuffs.
It must be your mother's. His voice warms up,
doing scales. Neck shivers like a bug's
inside it. Crack, the pavement pales and splits—
jackhammers like cicadas in the distance.

Measure a long time in one window frame
to the point where a feeling fell. A faded
palm outdistances the careful names
you chose for a daughter and a son, its shade
behaves outside of you, growing toward
late afternoon, a breeze pulls thoughts from one leaf
until it separates and settles for
a stone. You call ("no reason") your ex-wife
and tell her something small, about bus passes
for next fall, or some other obligation.

She's in another place. Another woman passes
the day asleep. A room away. The stations
are set in marble, but how far have you
moved? At all? Across a river. Brooklyn to
Manhattan. Some short interludes in France
where the world seemed closer to itself.
It remembers something that this land merely
echoes. It's all itinerancy here.
Cold planets counting for a few near holy
patterns somewhere above the interfering

Lamplight. Or look to them, in constellations
lit across windows. The imagination
falters at the numbers alive in their rooms.
Maybe, you think, you can enter another
through your own feeling, if it's deep enough.
It never is. The flesh on its scaffold holds
your hands, your voice, your instrument, your body;
all tuned for a sad sweet sad song,
but the figure of a sad man playing music
bends off key. Your fingers won't mend,
but really it's the mind that's rendered useless.
Tell me again when the performance ends.

The Landing: A Stage

Mine vater vas gebornen Im 19-
36. I guess the Germans own that year
(square root of which is 44).
Who cares. He fell off into the whitening
near 50, in the way an actor forges
or hangs his self on all his parts, and forgets
who is his and himself, and stands downstage
at the proscenium until we're quiet
in attention. Slow Hamlet gazed on
his father glazèd o'er in powd'ry chalk—
this means he is a ghost, though ghosts don't cough—
Dad's covered in it, talking in long moans,
each gesture casts a small flurry of white
into the lights, and the corpse-pantomime,

Belied by the solid body underneath,
can't last so long before that body's child.
He will return in a velvet shirt, with still
some baby powder on his collar, and
if I were older, I might say, "You still
have some of the ghost on your shoulder," as
I brush it off. Denmark would then become
Christopher Street, and we'd return home.
So partly is my youngest memory
of him, and part's a later dream. To be
old when he is still old. Still, I have Demark
like a ghost in my name. Chance has its role
keeping the little Russian-Jewish-Anglo
well covered in his Danish patronymic.

From what am I hanging? One moment on
a scaffold where life is playacting and
they all return from transient arrangements
of warm bodies, as if in a painting
that moves, and exit into life. And you
who often played the dead or those much older
than you ever reached, I have one more
of Shakespeare's pantomimes we never tried:
Edgar playing mad until his eyeless
father asks to be ushered off a cliff.
In speech the drop's only illusory.
The fall feels just like falling from your feet.
And I call you a feather, and recite:
"Thy life's a miracle. Speak yet again."

Mystery Plays

from the York Cycle

I. The Barkers' Play (12:66)

Dear light, scattered on your hat brim, come follow me into the
nearest garden.

The combed streets freshly tarred. Men in the trade winds shuffle
their cards.

A crescent is calmly forming where the barkers' play begins in the
devil-light

Of morning. Sound breaks on a hammer strike. A cowbell hangs from
the beginning

Tanner's wrist. Heaven is wheeled in. White leather draped over a
throne at its

Height. Wings held up on stakes. Flapping like flags in a puppet
country march.

Stay close to your mother. Those men in masks are real men. Just like
your father

Was when he played here. There's nothing to be afraid of. He only
talks that way.

The milk pale hand of the angel grays. *Harrow!* He falls from the air.
Sky's blank

Trapdoor. From heaven (the pageant wagon) down as a tumbler. Fast
into the dark

Free of glee. Thrown a glint in the round opened mouth. Murk mask
of the pavement

And crowd in domes above him. Umbrellas close with a cheer. The
devil's with us.

II. The Skinners' Play (19:50)

The plays swing full by noon. At the second station, where we

Sit on the scaffold before the Harphams' house, Micklegate

Road has disappeared in audience. The cycle's gone halfway

Through fall and fall, flood and birth and miracle. He rides

A donkey through all of us. A swelling path crowds, narrows,

And contracts. The players play us. Zacchaeus climbs above

Calling our birch a sycamore. He can see the wagon train grow

Heavy on its way from the priory. If he looks toward the Ouse,

The rest continue down stations. It keeps repeating: again

And again, equations set in motion, thinning past the bend.

Maybe by now, the angels fall a twelfth time at the Pavement.

If you could, like that child there climbing past the skirts

And sales carts, ducking under the low stride of the donkey;

If you could run nimbly across the bridge, through the curve

At Coney Street, cutting past the Wymans' garden for Common

Hall, up Stonegate, circling the city to its center, swift,

Unseen as a rabbit or mouse; if you knew the town since birth,

And if you were low enough and young—if you came this way, you

May see, in passing images, the whole story told backwards.

III. The Girdlers and Nailers' Play (11:38)

Father in a gown. A harp on his head. Those kids

Are eating chocolate pudding. A salesman in a

Motley suit, kiting off a mechanized falcon.

Who is light enough to be carried away on this?

Hands in the air, sleeves down the shoulders,

Spoons highest of all. The youngest searches

A booth above her head. Fingers blindly trace

Cool lead circles on a leash. She moves to a row

Of miniatures—a horse, a sheep, a foal, a cow—

All made of tin. She plucks them one by one, and

Tries them in her mouth. They taste like sand.

IV. The Chandlers' Play (6:36)

On the wall, a horse tied to a change-house,

Tiny. A candle in the glass above, its flame

The same burnt hay sloping across the whole

Encaustic pasture: snow patched, trees to

Hazel strings, a bird trap. Unpeopled now.

Three crooks lean against a flat muted sky.

V. The Fishers and Mariners' Play (10:34)

Saturn clinched sadly in his belt, like a

Sage's neglected boulder by a whetstone

Hunched, resting a sandwich on his round

Middle, like an old baby on a new one. From

A bowl of porridge, a great, cloth-brown

Pear in broth, the dumpling's ears float

Half to the palette and half to the copper

Basin. Seven doves caged in a hull coo for

Dough from the wagon's skirt. Their five

Brothers look down from the clerestory.

VI. The Pinners' Play (14:28)

Again, again the tree it bends, it

Shudders. Shut up already. Still

It. Four wedges will do. It's like

A table then? You're like a magpie

A jay. Babble babble. The mortise

Doesn't receive it like a tenon in

A dovetail. In, in, in, over, over

All this fitting for the pinners.

Tomorrow you'll be pined. How're

You using that? Tree-wise. Mad as

A kestrel's den. Lurk lurk, I say.

See the wagons are backed up again

Thanks to us. He's quiet, Steven.

He didn't wake when we lifted him?

VII. The Smiths' Play (8:40)

This tale is a train. A desert outline for a song.

Which way in white fool's cloth? To where the mad

Are forced to rhyme? Hang your stars on rafters.

And call it your cap. Wear the house on your head,

Too. The Judas tree blooms. The hunted galleons

Are blue, so invisible: ship, soap, wheel, rope

Foaming on the chin like a beast. Your daughter,

Stands there still, untouched like a lily at the

VIII. The Tapiters and Couchers' Play (13:33)

Feast. Where are we in time? I am Pilate.

The wife has gone to bed. Sentries fetch

Me wine. I've heard them say the vintage

Comes from a charmer. It helps the heavy

Things to float away. Mahound. All of us

Have a birth date. And, minutes in flesh

We'll say a word here when we shouldn't.

I see them on the hill, my theater of men.

A few words will matter, because most of

Us can only remember a few words. My wife

Warns of a lot of things: that something

Lives beneath her bed. Her head is far in

The woods. She is no Eve. But then who is?

IX. The Fullers' Play (21:21)

Hold it even as a line. Her

Shoulders gone under the

Lake then the head. Or was

It not the other way? Head

First she dove from a rock

Her hands before her, her

Arms unlocked, her feet,

Flat and kicking, all the

Way down. I don't know why

I mention this. She would

Wake us early. To be alone

At the lake. Her sweater,

Made fresh from fuller's

Earth, would carry light

Through the dim wood. How

The city square sits like

A lake being approached.

'Fore it's ready. I watch

An early, earthly pigeon

Sweep the ground glossed

In cobblestone ripples.

X. The Mercers' Play (18:38)

What is this? All these plays, and a different

Christ in each. Most actors are lousy drunks.

Most writers tools. It's just us fools. So why

All this? What do you think the theater brings

Back to you? I'd like to say the dead but really

What? What are you looking at? Are you inside?

Or out of doors? Who is there? (Answer me.) Who

When we stand at our small threshold: an arch,

Or star, or the proscenium blade above? Which

One will drop? The words, re-wombed and wound

Like a clock, they alone take hold of your body

In melody, sight, practice, memory. All drop

As they did before, a hundred times, hundreds

Of years ago. At times, my mother repeats them

Over the breakfast table, as if she's talking

To a man behind me. At times, she says them to me

As if I am that man or woman from the script. And

My father did the same. Who are they then? When

XI. The Butchers' Play (24:14)

Long Thursdays,

The bodies full.

Alehouses still

Flooded as games

Or plays wheel by

An eleventh time

For the station.

Will you let your

Head slip down to

Painted toes, or

St. Mary's Abbey

In a fallen state

Hollowing years

After bombings,

And be her ruins:

Dressed gaudily

In a gauze of past

Pageants? Sleep

Combs along your

Lash. Maybe here

Life will regain

Old forms before

You wake fast to a

Jarring prayer.

XII. The Tilethatchers' Play (16:36)

Roofless night. The tilethatchers rest in

The nativity hay. One clutches a sheep mask

To his chest and snores loudly. The dusting

Of sequins, mimic-starlight they had cast

Through the broken roof upon the toy child,

Reflects the actual moonlight moving over

The exposed stage. And now it is time for the

Wings. Sweeping dark fabric against a dark

Backdrop. Wheeling each sleeping scene to

The carriage houses. A boy holds his finger

And thumb over the tongue of a bell. Hushed,

He follows them in across one life bolted

To the doorway. Now is the time for putting

Everything away. Some bread carried off in

The beaks. Some sweepers again making wing

Noises or brushing bottles off of the curb.

III

ELEGY

I remember a tree of a painting.

My whiter rings worn poor from prayer.

Saturday, a fawn wing sung of women and of woods:

"We heap the pearls, we loose the ground,

and some go godward with a rose."

There sat a little man like a silver birth tree.

A crowd in my ear where a woman with love would mirth me.

Her voice sliding rum from a songbeaker

rang the rimed, gray, waned glass,

and sent me into a drying river.

My young hand in clay, I cocked the swan's neck,

and, as the old bearer brought to rest

in the tents of the trees, he spoke to me:

"O paint early with your young voice

in the boathouses, in a raft in July

where a man after fifty cups

cool reeds to his face, and knows

the harbor is sane. I am waiting hand

opened to you, a drink in the other,

and my head is sand."

And I said to him: "I remember you.

Sunday, a wife in your pupil,

white limbs in the kiln.

Why didn't they show you to us?

We were your children in the brush

and only on the canvas did we fold away

from your likeness into flux."

And said the swan:

"A mimic's feeling somewhere sad,

he speaks groundward

mouth on urn

grape broken tongue

and wild grow his bones."

We feed July to the geese

in jeweled wakes diverging, holding

the sky's cloth like a mast

while white clovers knot us to the past.